RECENT RESEARCHES IN THE MUSIC OF THE BAROQUE ERA, 168

Gottfried Heinrich Stölzel

German Te Deum

A Setting of Martin Luther's Translation

Edited by Melvin Unger

A-R Editions, Inc.

German Te Deum

RECENT RESEARCHES IN MUSIC

A-R Editions publishes seven series of critical editions, spanning the history of Western music, American music, and oral traditions.

RECENT RESEARCHES IN THE MUSIC OF THE MIDDLE AGES AND EARLY RENAISSANCE
    Charles M. Atkinson, general editor

RECENT RESEARCHES IN THE MUSIC OF THE RENAISSANCE
    James Haar, general editor

RECENT RESEARCHES IN THE MUSIC OF THE BAROQUE ERA
    Christoph Wolff, general editor

RECENT RESEARCHES IN THE MUSIC OF THE CLASSICAL ERA
    Neal Zaslaw, general editor

RECENT RESEARCHES IN THE MUSIC OF THE NINETEENTH AND EARLY TWENTIETH CENTURIES
    Rufus Hallmark, general editor

RECENT RESEARCHES IN AMERICAN MUSIC
    John M. Graziano, general editor

RECENT RESEARCHES IN THE ORAL TRADITIONS OF MUSIC
    Philip V. Bohlman, general editor

Each edition in *Recent Researches* is devoted to works by a single composer or to a single genre. The content is chosen for its high quality and historical importance and is edited according to the scholarly standards that govern the making of all reliable editions.

For information on establishing a standing order to any of our series, or for editorial guidelines on submitting proposals, please contact:

A-R Editions, Inc.
Middleton, Wisconsin

800 736-0070 (North American book orders)
608 836-9000 (phone)
608 831-8200 (fax)
http://www.areditions.com

RECENT RESEARCHES IN THE MUSIC OF THE BAROQUE ERA, 168

Gottfried Heinrich Stölzel

German Te Deum

A Setting of Martin Luther's Translation

Edited by Melvin Unger

A-R Editions, Inc.
Middleton, Wisconsin

For my parents, John and Susie Unger

Performance parts are available from the publisher.

A-R Editions, Inc., Middleton, Wisconsin
© 2010 by A-R Editions, Inc.

All rights reserved. No part of this book may be reproduced or transmitted in any form by any electronic or mechanical means (including photocopying, recording, or information storage and retrieval) without permission in writing from the publisher.

The purchase of this edition does not convey the right to perform it in public, nor to make a recording of it for any purpose. Such permission must be obtained in advance from the publisher.

A-R Editions is pleased to support scholars and performers in their use of *Recent Researches* material for study or performance. Subscribers to any of the *Recent Researches* series, as well as patrons of subscribing institutions, are invited to apply for information about our "Copyright Sharing Policy."

Printed in the United States of America

ISBN-13: 978-0-89579-677-6
ISBN-10: 0-89579-677-5
ISSN: 0484-0828

♾ The paper used in this publication meets the minimum requirements of the American National Standard for Information Sciences—Permanence of Paper for Printed Library Materials, ANSI Z39.48-1992.

Contents

Acknowledgments vi

Introduction vii
   The Composer vii
   Stölzel's Setting of the German Te Deum viii
   Notes xi

Text and Translation xiii

Plates xv

German Te Deum
    1. Herr Gott, dich loben wir 1
    2. Dich, Vater, in Ewigkeit 13
    3. Heilig ist unser Gott 16
    4. Dein göttlich Macht 33
    5. Die gantze werthe Christenheit 36
    6. Dich, Vater, im höchsten Thron 49
    7. Du Kön'g der Ehren 51
    8. Nun hilff uns, Herr 61
    9. Täglich, Herr Gott, wir loben dich 80
   10. Auf dich hoffen wir 83
   11. Amen 89

Critical Report
   Sources 111
   Editorial Methods 111
   Critical Notes 112

Acknowledgments

I am grateful to the Schlossmuseum of Sondershausen and its director, Christa Hirschler, for permission to publish this edition of Gottfried Heinrich Stölzel's German Te Deum, based on the score and performing parts residing in Sondershausen as Mus. A 15:3. Thanks are due also to Dr. Don Smithers for providing the Riemenschneider Bach Institute with microfilms of these manuscripts. It was in my capacity as Director of the Bach Institute that I had access to these sources.

Introduction

Gottfried Heinrich Stölzel (1690–1749) was regarded by his contemporaries as one of the greatest composers of his time. In 1739 the Societät der Musikalischen Wissenschaften, led by Lorenz Christoph Mizler (1711–78), elected him to membership. In 1751 Johann Scheibe (1708–76) heard some of his oratorios in Copenhagen.[1] Contemporary writings inevitably named him as a leading German composer. In 1756 Friedrich Wilhelm Marpurg (1718–95), identifying the most famous composers of the eighteenth century (not just Germans), listed Stölzel as no. 37 and Johann Sebastian Bach as no. 40.[2] Bach himself evidently valued Stölzel's music, for he included the Partita in G minor (adding his own trio to the minuet) in *Das Clavier-Büchlein vor Wilhelm Friedemann Bach* (1720) and performed some of Stölzel's church works in Leipzig—the Passion oratorio *Ein Lämmlein geht und träget die Schuld* on 23 April 1734[3] and a whole cantata cycle in 1735/36.[4]

Unfortunately, a large portion of Stölzel's substantial oeuvre has been lost, and few of the surviving works are readily available in modern edition. As a result, he is still relatively unknown today. Many of the extant works (especially cantatas) are preserved in the Schlossmuseum (Palace Museum) at Sondershausen, Germany. A few years ago the Riemenschneider Bach Institute had the good fortune of obtaining twenty-six reels of microfilm containing these pieces, among which is a German Te Deum. Its substantial duration, stylistic variety, and full orchestration (three high trumpets, timpani, oboe, strings, continuo, and concerted voices) make it a good introduction to the composer's early work.

The Composer

Stölzel was born on 13 January 1690 in Grünstädtel (near Schwarzenberg, Ore Mountains).[5] He received his first music training (in singing and keyboard playing) from his father, who was an organist. At age thirteen he entered the lyceum at Schneeberg, where he studied continuo playing and composition with the cantor Christian Umlauft, who had been a student of Johann Kuhnau (1660–1722). In 1707 he enrolled at the university in Leipzig to study theology but felt drawn to music. He encountered the compositions of Georg Philipp Telemann (1681–1767) and Melchior Hoffmann (ca. 1679–1715—director of the New Church and also of the collegium musicum originally founded by Telemann) and frequented the recently reopened opera, where dramatic works by these and other composers were being performed. Hoffmann encouraged the young composer and provided opportunity for some of his works to be performed at the church.

In 1710 he moved to Breslau (now Wrocław, Poland), where he spent over two years teaching singing and keyboard playing to members of the aristocracy. He also composed many instrumental pieces for the collegium musicum, a serenade in honor of the coronation of emperor Charles VI, and his first dramatic work, *Narcissus* (supplying both libretto and music).

A teacher of Italian in Breslau persuaded him to consider a trip to Italy. In preparation for the journey he traveled back to Saxony. There, through the negotiations of Johann Theile and Johann Friedrich Fasch (whom Stölzel knew from his Leipzig days), he received unexpected commissions from the Zeitz court to compose operas for the Naumburg fair (*Valeria*, 1712; *Artemisia* and *Orion*, 1713—all lost). For these productions he supplied both libretto and music. He also wrote a pastorale for the court at Gera as well as many other church and chamber works. Thereupon he received offers of the position of kapellmeister from both the Gera and Zeitz courts, but he declined in order to fulfill his wish to travel to Italy in 1713. On his way to Italy, he visited various German cities. In Venice, accompanied by fellow German composer Johann David Heinichen (1683–1729), he heard concerts at the conservatories and met many local composers including Francesco Gasparini (1661–1727) and Antonio Vivaldi (1678–1741). He went next to Florence, where he was a well-received guest of the court. A month-long stay in Rome was followed by a return to Florence.

After visiting some more Italian cities, he traveled via Innsbruck and Linz to Prague (1715), where he was very active for three years, composing dramatic works, oratorios, masses, and instrumental music. Some of his works were presented in public concerts. He declined an offer from the court at Dresden (which would have included a trip to France funded by the king). Instead he went to Bayreuth to fulfill a commission to produce music for the two hundredth anniversary celebration of the Lutheran Reformation (1717).[6] There he also wrote two serenades for the duke's birthday and an opera.

By 1718 he was court kapellmeister in Gera. That same year he applied for a position at the court in Sondershausen, which had been vacant since 1715. He was unsuccessful in his application, however, the position going instead to Johann Balthasar Christian Freißlich (1687–1764). Shortly thereafter Stölzel applied successfully for a similar position at Saxe-Gotha. The appointment was made on 24 February 1720, and Stölzel was to remain in Gotha until his death on 27 November 1749.

Stölzel's output in Gotha was prodigious. Although much of his oeuvre has been lost, it apparently included at least twelve liturgical cantata cycles (some of them double cycles), seven Passions, Latin church works, secular cantatas, eighteen dramatic works (operas, pastorales, etc., almost all with German libretti), and a great deal of chamber music.[7]

Stölzel was also known as a teacher, writer, and theorist. He often provided his own libretti for vocal works. His scholarly writings include a treatise on canon (published during his lifetime) and *Abhandlung vom Recitativ*, the first major treatise on recitative.

Although Stölzel did not travel much after his return from Italy, his reputation was widespread. Unfortunately, most of Stölzel's Gotha manuscripts are no longer extant, many of them discarded during the tenure of his successor, Georg Benda (1722–95).[8] Some of his pieces survive, however, in copies made for the court at Sondershausen. According to Ernst Ludwig Gerber, when Prince Günther I became more familiar with Stölzel's music, he regretted not having hired him for his court, but made up for his error by requesting copies of Stölzel's pieces, which the composer supplied after Johann Freißlich's departure from Sondershausen in 1732/33.[9] It is for this reason that the Sondershausen Palace Museum is now one of the most important repositories of Stölzel's music.

Stölzel's Setting of the German Te Deum

The Te Deum is regarded as one of the great canticles of the Christian Church, and a classic expression of faith since the time of Ambrose.[10] Martin Luther considered it equal to the liturgical confessions and translated it into German verse around 1529. This translation may have first appeared in Joseph Klug's Wittenberg hymnal of 1529 (now lost); the first extant source (where it appears with music) is Andreas Rauscher's *Gesangbuch Erfurt* (1531).[11] Although earlier prose and poetic translations had existed in Germany, Luther's version soon eclipsed them in hymnals of the time (see example 1).[12]

Stölzel's setting of the German Te Deum was likely written in 1717, when he was commissioned to produce music in Bayreuth for the two hundreth anniversary celebration of the Lutheran reformation. In a biographical entry for the composer, Johann Adam Hiller (1728–1804)—commenting on Stölzel's mastery of counterpoint ("gebundene Schreibart")—noted that the Te Deum contained "some well-developed fugues."[13] Throughout much of the piece, Stölzel follows Luther's tune and antiphonal structure,[14] but he foregoes Luther's tune in passages set (or at least begun) imitatively: "Heilig ist unser Gott" (mm. 75–195), "Die gantze werthe Christenheit" (mm. 217–48), "Nun hilff uns, Herr" (mm. 302–415), "Auf dich hoffen wir" (mm. 451–521), and "Amen" (mm. 522–87). Even in these imitative passages, however, he usually preserves Luther's antiphonal structure by alternating polyphonic statements with homophonic ones; an exception is the concluding "Amen."

Although Stölzel's Te Deum is clearly sectional, performances should take into account the underlying unity provided by Luther's tune. In accordance with the sources, individual sections in this edition are demarcated with double barlines.[15] It seems clear that the basic tempo should be derived from the tempo of the chorale tune (ca. seventy-two beats per minute for the underlying pulse, whether quarter or half note). Nevertheless, some sections may be taken faster or slower. Proposed tempi are given below.

Intonatio: Ad libitum
M. 1: Herr Gott, dich loben wir ($\quarter = 72$)
M. 38: Dich, Vater, in Ewigkeit ($\quarter = 72$)
M. 75: Heilig ist unser Gott ($\quarter = 72$)
M. 196: Dein göttlich Macht ($\quarter = 68$)
M. 217: Die gantze werthe Christenheit ($\quarter = 96$)
M. 249: Dich, Vater, im höchsten Thron ($\quarter = 72$)
M. 271: Du Kön'g der Ehren ($\quarter = 72$)
M. 302: Nun hilff uns, Herr ($\quarter = 72$)
M. 416: Täglich, Herr Gott, wir loben dich ($\quarter = 72$)
M. 451: Auf dich hoffen wir ($\quarter = 72$)
M. 522: Amen ($\quarter = 84$)

Certain aspects of the score and original parts (see critical report) suggest French influence, in particular, the five-part string writing resulting from two separate viola (alto viola and tenor viola) parts, and the use of *Tief Kammerton* (A-Kammerton) implied by the presence of a transposed organ part (notated a minor third below) in addition to an untransposed one. While *solo* and *tutti* markings appear mostly in the performing parts, both vocal and instrumental, they are not absent from the score (e.g., markings in the vocal lines at mm. 43, 48, 53, 58, 71), suggesting more than one singer per part, although the set of performing parts includes only one copy of each vocal part (see description of sources in the critical report). Similarly, *con organo* and *senz' org.* markings in the continuo line of the score indicate more than one continuo instrument, as do the multiple performing parts. Besides the two organ parts, the manuscript part set includes a continuo part and a basso part. In view of the French influence mentioned above one could even argue for doubling the basso with a bassoon, especially since the violin 1 part is already doubled by an oboe throughout much of the work.[16] The continuo part mirrors the continuo line of the score, including the *con organo* and *senz' org.* markings and directions for the basso to play *pizzicato* (mm. 416–49). Except for the transposition, the transposed organ part is identical, including all of the notes in measures 416–28, 431–35, 437–42, and 444–49, yet has *pizzicato senz' organo* and *con organo* at the respective junctures, perhaps suggesting that the scribe (not the same as that of the other organ part) based it on the continuo part rather than deriving it directly from the score. The continuo and transposed organ parts share some significant departures from the full score: they drop the upper voice in measures 218–19 (non-transposed

Example 1. Martin Luther, Te Deum (1531), after the transcription by Hans Joachim Moser in *D. Martin Luthers Werke: Kritische Gesamtausgabe*, vol. 35, *Die Lieder Luthers*, ed. W. Lucke (Weimar: Böhlau, 1923; repr., 2005), 521–24.

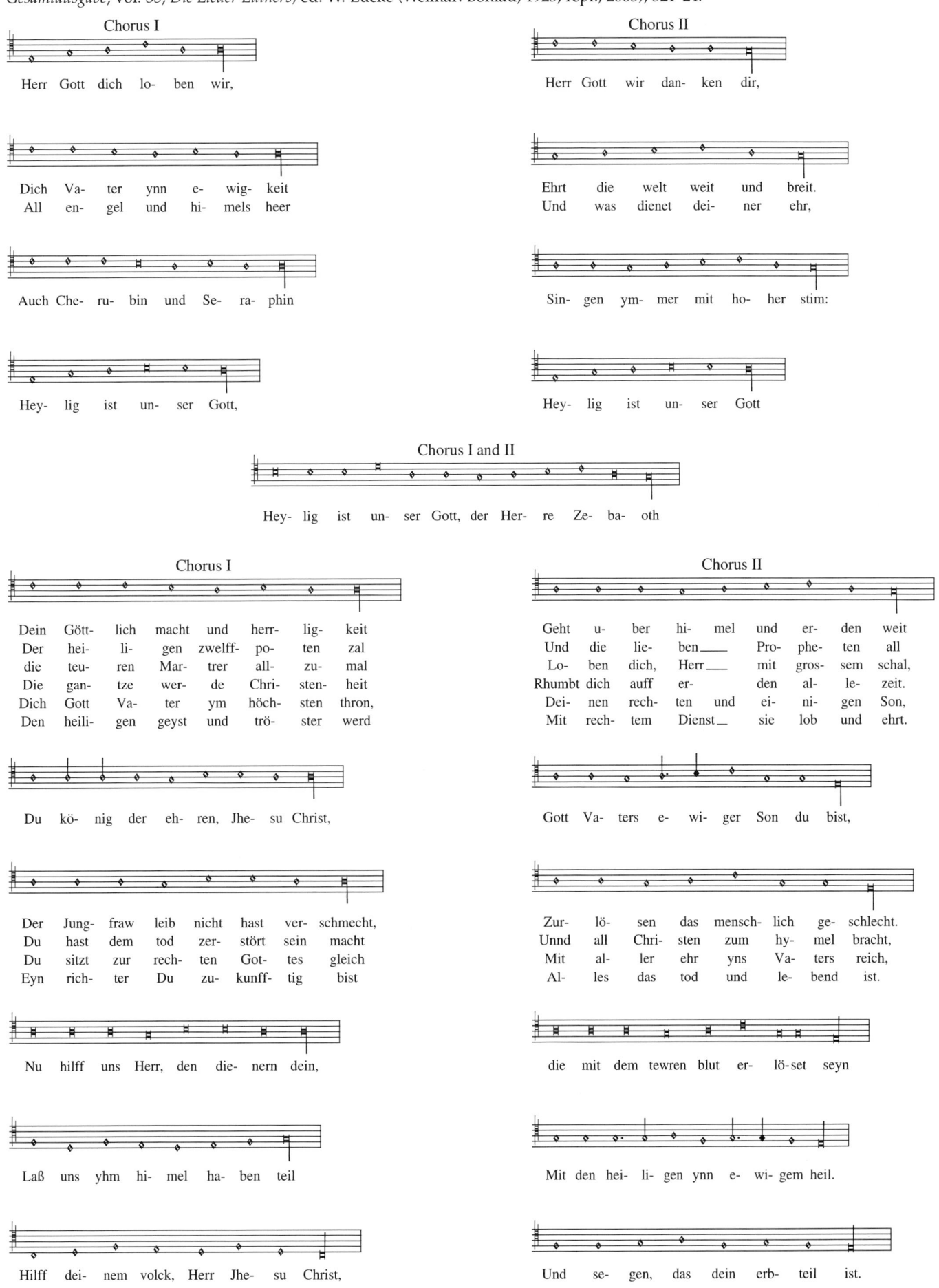

Example 1 continued

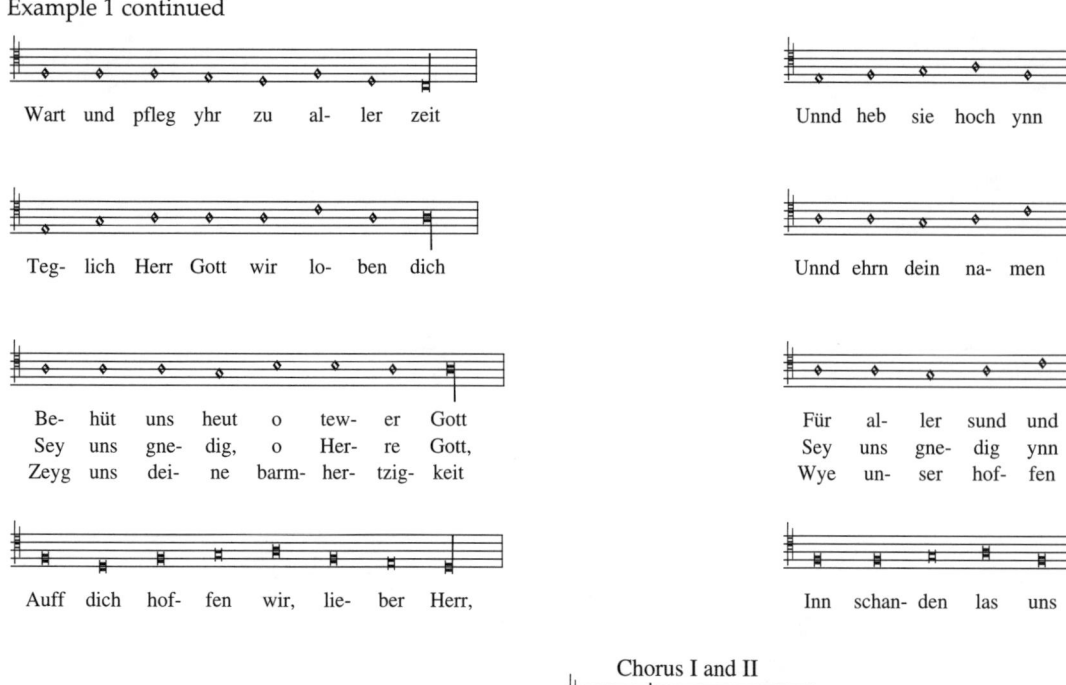

organ has both voices) and maintain the treble clef in measure 90 (score and non-transposed organ have soprano clef) and the bass clef in measure 525 (score and non-transposed organ have tenor clef). The non-transposed organ part, on the other hand, while identical to the continuo part (except for the above-mentioned departures, where it follows the continuo line of the score), does not include the directives *senz' organo* and *con organo*, instead simply dropping out for the respective measures (for numbers, see above). The basso part, which has no figures, drops out frequently. It does so in contrapuntal passages, whenever the continuo line doubles a vocal part other than the vocal bass (which has dropped out, too). This was common practice at the time, and is confirmed in the original continuo performing parts with changes of clef. The significance of this notational convention is explained by Johann Samuel Petri (1738–1808) in his *Anleitung zur praktischen Musik*: "One . . . should also note . . . that the violone player . . . ought to cease playing entirely as soon as tenor, alto, or discant clefs appear and to defer to the violoncellos until a bass clef recurs. Moreover, if composers wish the bass to sound high and soft, they often write 'Violoncelli,' or 'Violoncelli Soli,' whereby the violonist ceases playing until a 'Tutti' or 'Violone' marking recurs."[17] Thus it would seem that the violoncellist used the continuo rather than the basso part.

Unlike the set of Stölzel's cantatas recorded as a "Christmas Oratorio" by Ludger Rémy,[18] the present work keeps the voices within comfortable ranges, so a pitch of a′ = ca. 392 Hz (as preferred by Rémy) is unwarranted.

The oboe part is problematic. It doubles the first violin and extends below the range of the modern instrument. Such occurrences are not uncommon in music of the time. Typically such problems are solved by playing the part on an oboe d'amore, adjusting the intervals of the passage (*Knicken*), or omitting the lowest passages.[19] The latter two options are particularly appropriate in this case since the notes are played by the violin anyway.[20] Interestingly, in the Sondershausen performing part, the low a is usually avoided: either the part simply has a rest instead of the unplayable note (see mm. 74 and 270), or it is rewritten, using a′ instead of a. In one rare instance, c′ is substituted (m. 216). Still, this written-out *Knicken* has not been carried through systematically in the source, as can be seen in example 2, where the low a is left standing in measure 534, but eliminated in measure 535. In this edition, the low a has been eliminated throughout; the details of the editorial emendations are described in the critical notes.

Example 2. Gottfried Heinrich Stölzel, German Te Deum, oboe part according to manuscript part set, mm. 534–35.

Notes

1. *Die Musik in Geschichte und Gegenwart* (1949–86), s.v. "Stölzel, Gottfried Heinrich" (col. 1384), by Dieter Härtwig and Fritz Henneberg.

2. Werner Neumann and Hans-Joachim Schulze, eds., *Bach-Dokumente*, 4 vols. (Leipzig: Bach-Archiv, 1963, 1969, 1972, 1979), 3:116 (no. 687).

3. See Tatjana Schabalina [Tatiana Shabalina], "'Texte zur Music' in Sankt Petersburg. Neue Quellen zur Leipziger Musikgeschichte sowie zur Kompositions- und Aufführungstätigkeit Johann Sebastian Bachs," *Bach-Jahrbuch* 94 (2008): 77–84.

4. See Marc-Roderich Pfau, "Ein unbekanntes Leipziger Kantatentextheft aus dem Jahr 1735: Neues zum Thema Bach und Stölzel," *Bach-Jahrbuch* 94 (2008), 111–22. Furthermore, the aria "Bist du bei mir" (from Stölzel's 1718 opera *Diomedes oder die triumphierende Unschuld*) appears in the 1725 *Clavierbüchlein vor Anna Magdalena Bach* (copied by Anna Magdalena herself). See Andreas Glöckner, "Neues zum Thema Bach und die Oper seiner Zeit," *Bach-Jahrbuch* 92 (2002): 173–74.

5. Early sources for information about Stölzel include an autobiography in Johann Mattheson's *Grundlage einer Ehren-Pforte* (Hamburg, 1740) and Johann Adam Hiller, *Lebensbeschreibungen berühmter Musikgelehrten und Tonkünstler neuerer Zeit*, vol. 1 (Leipzig, 1784).

6. *The New Grove Dictionary of Music and Musicians*, 2nd ed. (hereafter *NG2*), s.v. "Stölzel, Gottfried Heinrich" (p. 434), by Fritz Hennenberg.

7. Ibid.

8. Fritz Hennenberg, *Das Kantatenschaffen von Gottfried Heinrich Stölzel*, Beiträge zur musikwissenschaftlichen Forschung in der DDR, vol. 8. (Leipzig: VEB Deutscher Verlag für Musik, 1976), 21.

9. Ernst Ludwig Gerber, *Historisch-Biographisches Lexicon der Tonkünstler* (Leipzig, 1790–92), s.v. "Stoelzel (Gottfried Heinrich)," col. 589. According to *NG2*, s.v. "Freißlich, Johann Balthasar Christian," by Paweł Podejko, Freißlich left Sondershausen around 1730.

10. According to medieval legend, Augustine and Ambrose sang the Te Deum in alternation as an improvised prayer at the baptism of Augustine by Ambrose. See *NG2*, s.v. "Te Deum" (p. 191), by Ruth Steiner and Keith Falconer.

11. For a scholarly edition with a discussion of all variants, see *D. Martin Luthers Werke: Kritische Gesamtausgabe*, vol. 35, *Die Lieder Luthers*, ed. W. Lucke (Weimar: Böhlau, 1923; repr. 2005), 249–54, 458–59, and 521–24; the last section includes a musical transcription by Hans Joachim Moser.

12. Ibid., 250–54.

13. Hiller, *Lebensbeschreibungen*, 264 ("etliche fleißig gearbeitete Fugen").

14. In contrast to Luther's version, Stölzel does not repeat the melodic phrases used for "Dich, Vater, . . . ehret die Welt" to set "All Engel . . . und was dienet" but moves on already to the following ones, which he then uses a second time to set the following lines of text ("Auch Cherubim . . . singen immer"). See *Die Lieder Luthers*, 522.

15. Although double barlines do not appear in the manuscript score at mm. 216 and 450, they do appear in some of the performing parts. Both score and parts have only a single barline at m. 301, which is reproduced in this edition.

16. James R. Anthony, review of *Médée*, by Marc-Antoine Charpentier, ed. Edmond Lemaître, *Music and Letters* 70 (1989): 140–41: "In French Baroque practice the outer voices of the five-part string orchestra were normally doubled by oboes and bassoons respectively, notwithstanding the general lack of such information in the original scores."

17. Quoted in Karl Hochreither, trans. Melvin Unger, *Performance Practice of the Instrumental-Vocal Works of Johann Sebastian Bach* (Lanham, Md.: Scarecrow Press, 2002), 115.

18. Gottfried Heinrich Stölzel, *Christmas Oratorio—Cantatas 6–10*, Weimarer Barockensemble conducted by Ludger Rémy (2000), CPO 999 735-2, compact disc.

19. See Hochreither, trans. Unger, *Performance Practice*, 81–82; in particular, see examples of *Knicken* on p. 81.

20. See Werner Neumann, *Handbuch der Kantaten Johann Sebastian Bachs*, 4th rev. ed. (Leipzig: Breitkopf & Härtel, 1971), 11; quoted in Hochreither, trans. Unger, *Performance Practice*, 82.

Text and Translation

This edition retains the orthography of the Sondershausen score. It is noteworthy that Stölzel's spellings are more modern than those of Luther's original text, some two hundred years earlier (see example 1 of introduction). Nevertheless, archaic German spellings still occur (in the order of appearance): *dancken, zwölff, gantze, verschmächt, zukünfftig, todt, hilff, seyn, Mißethat, sey, Barmhertzigkeit,* and of course all those that have *th* for *t* (such as *Bothen, theuren, Noth*), forms that remained in force until 1901. It should also be noted that while some words do not rhyme in modern standard German, they do so in Luther's native dialect (e.g., *Gott* and *Mißethat* or *Barmhertzigkeit* and *steht*).

Te Deum laudamus

Herr Gott, dich loben wir,
Herr Gott, wir dancken dir.

Dich, Vater, in Ewigkeit
ehret die Welt weit und breit.
All Engel und Himmels Heer
und was dienet deiner Ehr,
auch Cherubim und Seraphim
singen immer mit hoher Stimm:

Heilig ist unser Gott,
der Herre Zebaoth.

Dein göttlich Macht und Herrlichkeit
geht über Himml und Erden weit.
Der heiligen zwölff Bothen Zahl,
und die lieben Propheten all,
die theuren Märtrer allzumahl
loben dich, Herr, mit großem Schall.

Die gantze werthe Christenheit
rühmt dich auf Erden allezeit.

Dich, Vater, im höchsten Thron,
deinen rechten und eingen Sohn,
den heilgen Geist und Tröster werth
mit rechtem Dienst sie lobt und ehrt.

Du Kön'g der Ehren, Jesu Christ,
Gott Vaters ew'ger Sohn du bist,
der Jungfrau Leib nicht hast verschmächt,
zuerlösen das menschlich Geschlecht.
Du hast dem Tod zerstört sein Macht
und all Christen zum Himmel bracht.
Du sitzt zur Rechten Gottes gleich
mit aller Ehr ins Vaters Reich.
Ein Richter du zukünfftig bist
alles, was todt und lebend ist.

Lord God, we praise you,
Lord God, we thank you.

You, Father, throughout eternity
does the world glorify far and wide.
All the angels and heaven's host
and all that serves your glory,
the cherubim and seraphim also,
sing evermore with raised voice:

"Holy is our God,
the Lord Sabaoth."

Your divine power and glory
fill heaven and earth.
The holy company of the twelve apostles
and the dear prophets all,
the noble martyrs too,
praise you, Lord, with mighty sound.

All Christendom throughout the world
praises you on earth continually.

You, Father, on the throne most high,
your true and only Son,
also the Holy Ghost, the dear Comforter,
with true service, it praises and honors.

You, King of Glory, Jesus Christ,
eternal Son of God,
did not disdain the Virgin's womb
to redeem the human race.
You have destroyed the power of death
and brought all Christians to heaven.
You sit at the right hand of God
in the full glory of the Father's kingdom.
You are the one who will judge
all the living and the dead.

Nun hilff uns, Herr, den Dienern dein, die mit dein'm theuren Blut erlöset seyn. Laß uns im Himmel haben Theil mit den Heil'gen in ew'gem Heil. Hilff deinem Volk, Herr Jesu Christ, und segne, was dein Erbtheil ist, wart und pfleg ihr zu aller Zeit und heb sie hoch in Ewigkeit.	Therefore, Lord, help us, your servants, who have been redeemed with your precious blood. Let us have a part in heaven with the saints in eternal salvation. Help your people, Lord Jesus Christ, and bless your heritage. Tend and care for them evermore, and lift them up throughout eternity.
Täglich, Herr Gott, wir loben dich und ehrn dein Namen stetiglich. Behüt uns heut, o treuer Gott, vor aller Sünd und Mißethat. Sey uns gnädig, o Herre Gott, sey uns gnädig in aller Noth. Zeig uns deine Barmhertzigkeit, wie unser Hoffnung zu dir steht.	Day by day, we magnify you; and glorify your name continually. Guard us this day, O faithful God, from all sin and transgression. Have mercy upon us, O Lord God, have mercy upon us in all trouble. Show us your compassion for our hope is in you.
Auf dich hoffen wir, lieber Herr, in Schanden laß uns nimmermehr.	In you we hope, dear Lord; let us never be put to shame.
Amen.	Amen.

Plate 1. Gottfried Heinrich Stölzel, German Te Deum, manuscript score, Schlossmuseum Sondershausen, Thuringia, Germany, Mus. A 15:3, first page with title "Te Deum laudamus" and attribution "di Stoelzel." Used with permission.

Plate 2. Gottfried Heinrich Stölzel, German Te Deum, manuscript score, Schlossmuseum Sondershausen, Thuringia, Germany, Mus. A 15:3, last page (fol. 53r) with date, "Gotha den 9. Julÿ 1759." Used with permission.

Plate 3. Gottfried Heinrich Stölzel, German Te Deum, manuscript part set, Schlossmuseum Sondershausen, Thuringia, Germany, Mus. A 15:3, first page of Violino Concertato part. Used with permission.

German Te Deum

1. Herr Gott, dich loben wir

2. Dich, Vater, in Ewigkeit

64
Ob.
C
A
T
B
Vn. 1
Vn. 2
A. Va.
T. Va.
Cont.
[solo]
auch Che- ru- bim und Se- ra- phim
70
tutti
sin- gen im- mer mit ho- her Stimm:
[tutti]
sin- gen im- mer mit ho- her Stimm:
[tutti]
sin- gen im- mer mit ho- her Stimm:
[tutti]
sin- gen im- mer mit ho- her Stimm:
tutti
tutti

3. Heilig ist unser Gott

17

18

19

105
Ob.
Clno. 1
Clno. 2
Clno. 3
Timp.
C
Hei- lig ist un- ser Gott, der
A
-lig ist un- ser Gott, der Her- re Ze- - ba- oth, der
T
Her- re Ze- ba- oth. Hei-
B
Hei-
Vn. 1
Vn. 2
A. Va.
T. Va.
Cont.
5 6 6 7 6 2 6
-Basso
+Basso

111
Ob.
Clno. 1
Clno. 2
Clno. 3
Timp.
C
Her- re Ze- - ba- oth, der Her- re Ze- ba- oth, der
A
Her- re Ze- ba- oth. Hei- lig ist un- ser Gott, der
T
-lig ist un- ser Gott, hei- lig ist
B
-lig ist un- ser Gott, der Her- re Ze- - ba- oth, der
Vn. 1
Vn. 2
A. Va.
T. Va.
Cont.

117
Ob.
Clno. 1
Clno. 2
Clno. 3
Timp.
C
Her- re Ze- - - ba- oth, hei- lig ist
A
Her- re Ze- - - ba- oth,
T
un- ser Gott, der Her- re Ze- - ba- oth, hei- - lig,
B
Her- re Ze- - - ba- oth,
Vn. 1
Vn. 2
A. Va.
T. Va.
Cont.
4 2 6 4 2 6 7 6

23

129
Ob.
C
-oth, hei- lig ist un- ser
A
-oth, der Her- re Ze- ba- oth,
T
Gott, der Her- re Ze- - ba- oth, der Her- re Ze- ba-
B
hei- lig ist un- ser Gott, der Her- re Ze- - ba-
Vn. 1
Vn. 2
A. Va.
T. Va.
Cont.
+Basso
135
Ob.
C
Gott, der Her- re Ze- - ba- oth, der Her- re Ze- ba-
A
hei- lig ist un- ser Gott, der Her- re Ze- - ba-
T
-oth, hei- lig ist un- ser
B
-oth, hei- lig ist un- ser
Vn. 1
Vn. 2
A. Va.
T. Va.
Cont.
-Basso
+Basso

141
Ob.
C
-oth, der Her- re Ze- ba- oth.
A
-oth, der Her- re Ze- ba- oth.
T
Gott, der Her- re Ze- ba- oth.
B
Gott, der Her- re Ze- ba- oth.
Vn. 1
Vn. 2
A. Va.
T. Va.
Cont.
147
Ob.
Clno. 1
Vn. 1
Vn. 2
A. Va.
T. Va.
Cont.
-Basso

26

159
Ob.
Clno. 1
Clno. 2
Clno. 3
Timp.
C
Ze- ba- oth, hei- lig ist
A
Ze- ba- oth, der Her- re Ze- ba- oth, der Her- re
T
un- ser Gott, der Her- re Ze- - ba- oth, der Her- re
B
hei- lig ist un- ser Gott, der Her- re Ze-
Vn. 1
Vn. 2
A. Va.
T. Va.
Cont.
7 7 6 7 7 7 ♯ 6 9 8

28

29

177
Ob.
Clno. 1
Clno. 2
Clno. 3
Timp.
C
hei- lig ist un- ser Gott, der Her- re Ze- - ba- oth, hei-
A
der Her- re Ze- ba- oth,
T
der Her- re Ze- ba- oth,
B
Gott, der Her- re Ze- - ba- oth, der Her- re Ze- ba- oth,
Vn. 1
Vn. 2
A. Va.
T. Va.
Cont.
7 6 6 6 5 ♯ 6 7 7

31

32

4. Dein göttlich Macht

203
Ob.
C
Himml und Er- den weit.
A
Himml und Er- den weit.
T
Himml und Er- den weit. Der hei- li- gen zwölff Bo- then
B
Himml und Er- den weit.
Vn. 1
Vn. 2
A. Va.
T. Va.
Cont.
207
Ob.
C
und die lie- ben Pro- phe- ten
A
und die lie- ben Pro- phe- ten
T
Zahl, und die lie- ben Pro- phe- ten
B
und die lie- ben Pro- phe- ten
Vn. 1
Vn. 2
A. Va.
T. Va.
Cont.

210
Ob.
C
A
T
B
Vn. 1
Vn. 2
A. Va.
T. Va.
Cont.
all,
all,
all, die theuren Märtrer allzumahl
all,
214
lo- ben dich, Herr, mit gro- ßem Schall.
lo- ben dich, Herr, mit gro- ßem Schall.
lo- ben dich, Herr, mit gro- ßem Schall.
lo- ben dich, Herr, mit gro- ßem Schall.

5. Die gantze werthe Christenheit

221
Ob.
Clno. 1
Clno. 2
Clno. 3
Timp.
C
al- le- zeit, rühmt dich auf Er-
A
al- le- zeit, rühmt dich auf Er- den
T
Die gan- tze wer- the Chri- sten- heit rühmt dich auf Er-
B
Er- - den al- le-
Vn. 1
Vn. 2
A. Va.
T. Va.
Cont.

38

39

228
Ob.
Clno. 1
Clno. 2
Clno. 3
Timp.
C
-le, al- le- zeit,
A
- le- zeit,
T
- le- zeit, die gan- tze
B
- den al- le- zeit,
Vn. 1
Vn. 2
A. Va.
T. Va.
Cont.
5 6 4 2 6

230
Ob.
C
die gan- tze wer- the Chri- sten- heit rühmt dich auf Er- den_ al- le- zeit,
A
die gan- tze wer- the Chri- sten- heit rühmt dich auf Er- den al- le- zeit, die gan- tze
T
wer- the Chri- sten- heit,
B
die gan- tze wer- the Chri- sten- heit rühmt dich auf Er- den, rühmt dich auf Er- den,
Vn. 1
Vn. 2
A. Va.
T. Va.
Cont.
232
Ob.
C
die gan- tze wer- the Chri- sten- heit rühmt dich auf Er- den_ al- le- zeit,
A
wer- the Chri- sten- heit,
T
die gan- tze wer- the Chri- sten- heit rühmt dich auf Er- den al- le- zeit, die gan- tze
B
die gan- tze wer- the Chri- sten- heit rühmt dich auf Er- den al- le- zeit,
Vn. 1
Vn. 2
A. Va.
T. Va.
Cont.

234
Ob.
Clno. 1
Clno. 2
Clno. 3
Timp.
C
die gan- tze wer- the Chri- sten- heit rühmt dich auf Er- den al- le- zeit, al-
A
die gan- tze wer- the Chri- sten- heit rühmt dich auf Er- den al-
T
wer- the Chri- sten- heit rühmt dich auf Er- den
B
die gan- tze wer- the Chri- sten- heit rühmt dich auf Er- den al-
Vn. 1
Vn. 2
A. Va.
T. Va.
Cont.

43

44

240
Ob.
Clno. 1
Clno. 2
Clno. 3
Timp.
C
al- le- zeit, al- le- zeit,
A
Er- den al- le- zeit, die gan- tze wer- the
T
Er- den, die gan- tze wer- the Chri- sten- heit rühmt dich auf Er-
B
Er- den al- le- zeit,
Vn. 1
Vn. 2
A. Va.
T. Va.
Cont.

46

244
Ob.
Clno. 1
Clno. 2
Clno. 3
Timp.
C
-le, al- le- zeit,
A
al- le- zeit,
T
Er- den al- le- zeit,
B
al- le- zeit,
Vn. 1
Vn. 2
A. Va.
T. Va.
6 7 6
Cont.

246
Ob.
Clno. 1
tr
Clno. 2
Clno. 3
Timp.
C
al- le, al- le- zeit.
A
al- le, al- le- zeit.
T
al- le, al- le- zeit.
B
al- le, al- le- zeit.
Vn. 1
Vn. 2
A. Va.
T. Va.
Cont.
6 5 5 4 3

6. Dich, Vater, im höchsten Thron

Dich, Va-ter, im höch-sten Thron, dei-nen rech-ten und

(A) dei-nen rech-ten und

(T) dei-nen rech-ten und

(B) dei-nen rech-ten und

259
Ob.
C
A
T
B
Vn. 1
Vn. 2
A. Va.
T. Va.
Cont.
ein- gen Sohn,
den heil- gen Geist und
ein- gen Sohn,
ein- gen Sohn,
ein- gen Sohn,
265
Trö- ster werth mit rech- tem Dienst sie lobt und ehrt.
mit rech- tem Dienst sie lobt und ehrt.
mit rech- tem Dienst sie lobt und ehrt.
mit rech- tem Dienst sie lobt und ehrt.

7. Du Kön'g der Ehren

Du Kön'g der Ehren, Je- su

275
Ob.
Clno. 1
Clno. 2
Clno. 3
Timp.
C
Gott Va- ters ew'- ger Sohn du bist,
A
Gott Va- ters ew'- ger Sohn du bist,
T
Christ, Gott Va- ters ew'- ger Sohn du bist,
B
Gott Va- ters ew'- ger Sohn du bist,
Vn. 1
Vn. 2
A. Va.
T. Va.
Cont.

53

der Jung- fraun Leib nicht hast ver-

54

zuer- lö- sen das mensch- lich Ge- schlecht. (C)

zuer- lö- sen das mensch- lich Ge- schlecht. (A)

-schmächt, zuer- lö- sen das mensch- lich Ge- schlecht. (T)

zuer- lö- sen das mensch- lich Ge- schlecht. (B)

Du hast dem Tod zer- stört sein

C: und all____ Chri- sten zum Him- mel bracht.

A: und all Chri- sten zum__ Him- mel bracht.

T: Macht und all Chri- sten zum Him- mel bracht.

B: und all Chri- sten zum__ Him- mel bracht.

[Basso]

57

Du sitzt zur Rech- ten Got- tes

mit aller Ehr ins Vaters Reich.

mit aller Ehr ins Vaters Reich.

gleich mit aller Ehr ins Vaters Reich.

mit aller Ehr ins Vaters Reich.

Ein Rich- ter du zu- künff- tig

299
Ob.
Clno. 1
Clno. 2
Clno. 3
Timp.
C
al- les, was todt und le- bend ist.
A
al- les, was todt und le- bend ist.
T
bist al- les, was todt und le- bend ist.
B
al- les, was todt und le- bend ist.
Vn. 1
Vn. 2
A. Va.
T. Va.
Cont.

8. Nun hilff uns, Herr

C: den Die - nern dein,

A: den Die - nern, den Die- nern dein,

T: Herr, den Die- nern dein, den Die- nern dein,

B: Nun hilff uns, Herr, den Die- nern dein,

63

318
Ob.
Clno. 1
Clno. 2
Clno. 3
Timp.
C
Laß uns im
A
Laß uns im Him- mel ha-
T
Laß uns im Him- mel ha- ben Theil, laß uns im
B
uns im Him- mel ha- ben Theil, laß uns im Him- mel ha-
Vn. 1
Vn. 2
A. Va.
T. Va.
Cont.

325

Lyrics (C, T): Him- mel ha- ben Theil mit den Heil'- gen in ew'- gem

Lyrics (A, B): - ben Theil mit den Heil'- gen in ew'- gem

331
Ob.
Clno. 1
Clno. 2
Clno. 3
Timp.
C
Heil.
A
Heil. Hilff dei- nem Volk,___ Herr___ Je- su___ Christ, Herr Je- su
T
Heil. Hilff dei- nem Volk,___ Herr Je-
B
Heil. Hilff dei- nem
Vn. 1
Vn. 2
A. Va.
T. Va.
Cont.
6 6 6 7 ♮5
-Basso
+Basso

337
Ob.
Clno. 1
Clno. 2
Clno. 3
Timp.
C
Hilff dei- nem Volk, Herr Je- su Christ,
A
Christ, hilff dei- nem Volk, Herr Je- su Christ,
T
- - - - su Christ,
B
Volk, Herr Je- - - su Christ,
Vn. 1
Vn. 2
A. Va.
T. Va.
Cont.

68

349
Ob.
Clno. 1
Clno. 2
Clno. 3
Timp.
C
wart und pfleg ihr zu al- ler
A
wart und pfleg ihr zu al- ler Zeit, wart und pfleg
T
ihr zu al- ler Zeit, zu al- ler Zeit, wart und pfleg
B
wart und pfleg
Vn. 1
Vn. 2
A. Va.
T. Va.
Cont.
-Basso
+Basso

Zeit,— zu al- ler Zeit, und heb sie hoch,

ihr zu al- ler Zeit, und heb sie hoch,

ihr zu al- ler Zeit, und heb sie hoch,

ihr— zu al- ler Zeit, und heb sie hoch,

71

366
Ob.
Clno. 1
Clno. 2
Clno. 3
Timp.
C
- wig- keit, in E- wig- keit, und heb sie
A
E- wig- keit, in E- - wig- keit, und heb sie hoch, und heb
T
und heb sie hoch in E- wig-
B
und heb sie hoch, in E-
Vn. 1
Vn. 2
A. Va.
T. Va.
Cont.
+Basso

372
Ob.
Clno. 1
Clno. 2
Clno. 3
Timp.
C
hoch, und heb sie hoch in E- - -
A
sie hoch, und heb sie hoch in E- - wig- keit, und heb
T
-keit, in E- - - - -
B
- wig- keit, und heb sie hoch in E- - wig- keit, in
Vn. 1
Vn. 2
A. Va.
T. Va.
Cont.

74

und heb sie hoch in E- - wig- keit, und heb

76

397
Ob.
Clno. 1
Clno. 2
Clno. 3
Timp.
C
- - wig- keit, in E- wig- keit, und
A
- - wig- keit, in E- - wig- keit, und heb
T
- - wig- keit, in E- wig- keit, und heb sie hoch
B
- - wig- keit, in E- wig- keit, und heb sie
Vn. 1
Vn. 2
A. Va.
T. Va.
Cont.

78

und heb sie hoch, in E- wig- keit.

9. Täglich, Herr Gott, wir loben dich

426
Ob.
C
Gott, wir lo- ben dich und ehrn dein Na- men ste- tig- lich.
A
und ehrn dein Na- men ste- tig- lich.
T
und ehrn dein Na- men ste- tig- lich.
B
und ehrn dein Na- men ste- tig- lich.
Vn. 1
con l'arco
pizz.
Vn. 2
con l'arco
pizz.
A. Va.
con l'arco
pizz.
T. Va.
[con l'arco]
Cont.
6
6
pizz.
con organo
senza organo
431
Ob.
C
Be- hüt uns heut, o treu- er Gott, vor al- ler
A
vor al- ler
T
vor al- ler
B
vor al- ler
Vn. 1
con l'arco
Vn. 2
con l'arco
A. Va.
con l'arco
T. Va.
[con l'arco]
Cont.
[con l'arco]
6
con organo

436
Ob.
C
Sünd und Mis- se- that.
Sey uns gnä- dig, o Her- re
A
Sünd und Mis- se- that.
T
Sünd und Mis- se- that.
B
Sünd und Mis- se- that.
Vn. 1
pizz.
Vn. 2
pizz.
A. Va.
[pizz.]
T. Va.
Cont.
6 6
pizz.
senza organo
441
Ob.
C
Gott, sey uns gnä- dig in al- ler Noth.
A
sey uns gnä- dig in al- ler Noth.
T
sey uns gnä- dig in al- ler Noth.
B
sey uns gnä- dig in al- ler Noth.
Vn. 1
con l'arco
pizz.
Vn. 2
con l'arco
pizz.
A. Va.
con l'arco
pizz.
T. Va.
[con l'arco]
Cont.
[con l'arco]
6 6 6
pizz.
con organo
senza organo

10. Auf dich hoffen wir

458
Ob.
C
dich hof- fen wir, lie- - ber, lie- ber Herr, in Schan- den
A
dich hof- fen wir, lie- - ber, lie- ber Herr, in Schan- den
T
lie- ber, lie- - ber, lie- ber Herr,
B
-fen wir, lie- ber, lie- ber, lie- - ber Herr,
Vn. 1
Vn. 2
A. Va.
T. Va.
Cont.
-Basso
465
Ob.
C
laß uns nim- mer- mehr, auf dich hof- fen wir, lie-
A
laß uns nim- mer- mehr, auf dich hof- fen wir, lie- ber Herr, lie-
T
auf dich hof- fen wir, lie- - -
B
auf dich hof- fen wir, lie- ber, lie-
Vn. 1
Vn. 2
A. Va.
T. Va.
Cont.
+Basso

472
Ob.
C
- ber, lie- ber Herr, auf dich hof- fen wir, lie- ber, lie-
A
- - ber Herr, auf dich hof- fen wir, lie- ber
T
- ber, lie- ber Herr, auf dich hof- fen wir, lie- ber,
B
- - ber Herr, auf dich hof- fen wir, lie- ber, lie-
Vn. 1
Vn. 2
A. Va.
T. Va.
Cont.
479
Ob.
C
- - ber Herr, in Schan- - - -
A
Herr, lie- - ber Herr, in Schan- - -
T
Herr, lie- - ber Herr, in Schan- - -
B
- - ber Herr, in Schan- - -
Vn. 1
Vn. 2
A. Va.
T. Va.
Cont.

486
Ob.
C
- den laß uns nim- mer- mehr, in Schan- den laß uns nim- mer-
A
- den laß uns nim- mer- mehr, in Schan- den laß uns nim- mer-
T
- den laß uns nim- mer- mehr, auf
B
- den laß uns nim- mer- mehr,
Vn. 1
Vn. 2
A. Va.
T. Va.
Cont.
-Basso
493
Ob.
C
-mehr, auf dich hof- fen wir, lie- - ber Herr, lie-
A
-mehr, auf dich hof- fen wir, lie- - ber Herr, lie- - ber
T
dich hof- fen wir, lie- ber Herr, auf dich hof- fen wir, lie- ber
B
auf dich hof- fen wir, lie- ber Herr, auf dich hof- fen wir,
Vn. 1
Vn. 2
A. Va.
T. Va.
Cont.
+Basso

500
Ob.
C
- ber Herr, in Schan- - - den laß uns nim- mer-
A
Herr, lie- - ber Herr, in Schan- - den laß uns nim- mer-
T
Herr, in Schan- - - - den, laß uns nim- mer-
B
lie- ber Herr, in Schan- - den laß uns nim- mer-
Vn. 1
Vn. 2
A. Va.
T. Va.
Cont.
507
Ob.
C
-mehr, auf dich hof- fen wir, lie- - ber Herr, lie-
A
-mehr, auf dich hof- fen wir, lie- ber Herr, auf dich hof- fen wir,
T
-mehr, auf dich hof- - fen, auf dich hof- fen wir, lie- ber,
B
-mehr, auf dich hof- fen wir, lie- - ber Herr, lie- - ber
Vn. 1
Vn. 2
A. Va.
T. Va.
Cont.

514
Ob.
Clno. 1
Clno. 2
Clno. 3
Timp.
C
- ber Herr, in Schan- - - den laß uns nim- mer- mehr.
A
lie- ber Herr, in Schan- - - den laß uns nim- mer- mehr.
T
lie- ber Herr, in Schan- - - den laß uns nim- mer- mehr.
B
Herr, lie- - ber Herr, in Schan- - den laß uns nim- mer- mehr.
Vn. 1
Vn. 2
A. Va.
T. Va.
Cont.
♯ 6 2 6 7 6 7 ♯ 5 6 5 ♯

11. Amen

526
Ob.
Clno. 1
Clno. 2
tr
Clno. 3
Timp.
C
a- men, a- men, a- -
A
a- men, a- men, a- men,
T
a- men, a- men, a- men,
B
A- men, a- men,
Vn. 1
Vn. 2
A. Va.
T. Va.
Cont.
7 6 6 7 6
+Basso
-Basso

529
Ob.
Clno. 1
Clno. 2
Clno. 3
Timp.
C
- men, a- - -
A
a- men, a- - men, a- men,
T
a- men, a- men, a-
B
a- men, a- men, a- -
Vn. 1
Vn. 2
A. Va.
T. Va.
Cont.
7 6 6 7 6 6
+Basso

532
Ob.
Clno. 1
Clno. 2
Clno. 3
Timp.
C
- men, a- men, a- men, a- - men, a- men, a-
A
a- men, a- - men, a- men, a-
T
- men, a- - men, a- men, a-
B
- men, a- men, a- men, a-
Vn. 1
Vn. 2
A. Va.
T. Va.
Cont.
4 2 6 ♮5 6 7 6 6 6

535
Ob.
p
f
Clno. 1
Clno. 2
Clno. 3
Timp.
C
- men, a- - men, a-
A
- men, a- men, a- men, a- men, a- -
T
p
f
- men, a- - men, a- men, a-
B
- men, a- - men, a-
Vn. 1
p
f
Vn. 2
A. Va.
T. Va.
p
f
Cont.
6 6 6 5 4 3 7 ♮5 4 3 3 7 ♮5
6 4 3
p
-Basso
f
+Basso

94

95

544
Ob.
Clno. 1
Clno. 2
Clno. 3
f
Timp.
C
a- men, a- men, a-
A
a- men, a- men, a- - men, a-
T
a- men, a- - men,
B
a- men, a- men, a- men, a- -
Vn. 1
Vn. 2
A. Va.
T. Va.
Cont.
7 6 7 6 6 4 3

547
Ob.
Clno. 1
Clno. 2
Clno. 3
Timp.
C
-men, a- - -
A
- men, a- -
T
a- - -
B
- - -
Vn. 1
Vn. 2
A. Va.
T. Va.
5 4 3 5 4 3 5 4 3 7 6 7 ♯ 6 5 ♯
Cont.

550
Ob.
Clno. 1
Clno. 2
Clno. 3
Timp.
C
-men, a- men, a- - men, a- - men, a-
A
-men, a- men, a- - men, a- men, a- men, a- men, a-
T
-men, a- men, a- - men, a- - men,
B
-men, a- men, a- - men, a- - men,
Vn. 1
Vn. 2
A. Va.
T. Va.
Cont.
-Basso

553
Ob.
Clno. 1
Clno. 2
Clno. 3
Timp.
C
- - - men, a-
A
-men, a- - men, a-
T
a- men, a- men, a-
B
a- men, a- -
Vn. 1
Vn. 2
A. Va.
T. Va.
Cont.
+Basso

556
Ob.
Clno. 1
Clno. 2
Clno. 3
Timp.
C
- - men, a- -
A
- - men, a- men, a-
T
- - men,
B
- - men,
Vn. 1
Vn. 2
A. Va.
T. Va.
Cont.
-Basso

559
Ob.
Clno. 1
Clno. 2
Clno. 3
Timp.
C
-men, a- men, a- men, a- - men,
A
-men, a- men, a- men, a- - men, a- men, a- men, a-
T
a- men, a- men, a- men, a- men, a-
B
a- men, a-
Vn. 1
Vn. 2
A. Va.
T. Va.
Cont.
6 7 6 6 7 6
+Basso

562
Ob.
Clno. 1
Clno. 2
Clno. 3
Timp.
C
a- men, a- men, a- men, a- men, a-
A
- men, a- men, a- men, a- -
T
- - men,
B
-men, a- men, a- men, a- -
Vn. 1
Vn. 2
A. Va.
T. Va.
Cont.
7 6 6 3 2 6 ♮5

103

568
Ob.
Clno. 1
Clno. 2
Clno. 3
Timp.
C
-men, a- men, a-
A
- men, a- men, a- men,
T
-men, a- men, a- men, a- - - men, a- men,
B
- men, a- men, a- men, a-
Vn. 1
Vn. 2
A. Va.
T. Va.
Cont.

105

106

577
Ob.
Clno. 1
Clno. 2
Clno. 3
Timp.
C
- men, a- - - men,
A
- men, a- - men, a- - men, a-
T
- men, a- men, a- men, a- - men,
B
- men, a- - men,
Vn. 1
Vn. 2
A. Va.
T. Va.
Cont.
6 7 ♮5 7 5 4 3
-Basso
+Basso

580
Ob.
Clno. 1
Clno. 2
Clno. 3
Timp.
C
a- men, a- men, a- - men, a-
A
-men, a- men, a- men, a- men, a-
T
a- men, a- men,
B
a- men, a- men, a-
Vn. 1
Vn. 2
A. Va.
T. Va.
tasto solo
Cont.

583
Ob.
Clno. 1
Clno. 2
Clno. 3
Timp.
C
-men, a- men, a- men, a- - men.
tr
A
- men, a- men, a- men, a- men.
T
a- men, a- men, a- - men.
B
- men, a- men, a- - men.
Vn. 1
Vn. 2
A. Va.
T. Va.
Cont.
6
5
4
3

Critical Report

Sources

The present edition is based upon the score and parts residing in the Schlossmuseum (Palace Museum) of Sondershausen, Thuringia, Germany, under the shelfmark Mus. A 15:3. The score comprises 125 folios plus title page. Its title page is inscribed "Te Deum Lau . . | damus" and has two shelfmarks at the bottom, "[Hs M11: LXXVI.]" and "Mus. A 15:3"; it appears that the bracketed shelfmark was superseded by the other, current one. The first page of the music (see plate 1) repeats the title, "Te Deum laudamus," and attributes the work "di Stoelzel." The staves are marked thus: Clarino 1, Clarino 2, Clarino 3, Tympani, Violino 1 & Oboe, Violino 2, Alto Viola, Tenore Viola, Canto, Alto, Tenore, Bass, Cont[inuo]; one of the first violins is later used as a solo instrument, marked "Violino Concertato" (first in m. 38). The performing parts, which have neither a wrapper cover nor a separate shelfmark, are marked—in the order of the score—as follows: Clarino 1mo, Clarino 2do, Clarino Terzo, Tÿmpani, Oboe, Violino Concertato, Violino i^{mo}, Violino 2, Alto Viola, Tenore Viola, Soprano, Alto, Tenore, Basso [vocal bass], Basso [instrumental bass], Continuo, Organo [two alternate parts, one of them notated a minor third lower]. Neither the score, dated "Gotha den 9 Julÿ 1759" and accompanied by the inscription "Soli Deo gloria," nor the parts appear to be autograph; for comparison, see the example of Stölzel's hand provided in *Die Musik in Geschichte und Gegenwart* (1949–86), s.v. "Stölzel, Gottfried Heinrich" (cols. 1379–80), by Dieter Härtwig and Fritz Henneberg.

Two additional manuscript copies of the work reside in the Staatsbibliothek zu Berlin – Preußischer Kulturbesitz. A comparison of these sources with the ones in Sondershausen suggests that one of them (Amalia B. 372, titled "Herr Gott dich loben wir von Stoelzel") appears to be a duplicate of the Sondershausen sources, the other (Mus.ms.21 410, titled "Te Deum deutsch dol sigl. Stoeltzel"), a reduction/transformation of the Sondershausen copies. Neither are dated. Interestingly, it appears that the handwriting of the revised Berlin score is very similar to (if not identical with) Stölzel's handwriting. Nevertheless, since the Sondershausen version exists in both score *and* parts, and since Mus.ms. 21 410 represents a simplified version, I have chosen to follow the Sondershausen materials.

Editorial Methods

In the sources, individual sections do not carry subtitles, though they are usually separated with double barlines. For ease of reference, numbered editorial section labels have been added in this edition. Modern score order has been adopted. The labels of the full score have been preferred over those of the parts; thus, the topmost vocal part is called "canto" rather than "soprano." Separate staves are not used for either the solo violin (Violino Concertato), which is included with the violin 1 part, or the basso and organ parts, which join the continuo line unless indicated otherwise.

The canto, alto, and tenor parts have been changed from C clefs to G clefs. The original clefs for alto and tenor violas have been retained. In the continuo lines of the original, clef changes occur when the vocal bass line falls silent and the continuo doubles the lowest sounding part. (Such passages sometimes have figures despite the use of C clefs.) These lines have been set in treble or bass clefs in the score, with scoring changes indicated above the staff where appropriate. In the continuo performing parts, some of the higher passages have been converted to tenor clef for the convenience of the cellist. The timpani part, originally rendered as a transposed part (notated in C, like the clarini, a tone lower than sounding pitch) has been moved to concert pitch.

Key signatures have been modernized, that is, the accidentals are placed on the lines or spaces according to current usage. Meter signatures are those of the source.

Notes are grouped and beamed in logical, recognizable units, usually reflecting the basic patterns of the original score. Notes in vocal lines are flagged and beamed according to syllabification and editorial slurs are given as broken lines.

In the sources, whole notes are used to signify notes occupying entire measures regardless of their actual duration. Where these do not add up to the rhythmic total of a measure in a given time signature (e.g., a whole note for one measure of $\frac{6}{4}$ meter, or a whole rest used for a half measure when that measure is divided across a system break), the note and rest values have been adjusted according to modern usage. The sources omit barlines when a new clef is introduced. Such notational peculiarities have been changed to modern conventions without notice.

Ties and slurs have been treated as closely as possible to the original. Where ties appear in the sources because measures are divided across a system break, the notes have been rewritten as longer values without notice. Where dotted notes are used in the sources for rhythmic values that cross barlines the notation has been modernized without comment.

Trills and ornamental notes have been included where they appear in the score and/or performing part. Editorial trills appear in brackets. Accents and articulations follow the original. Editorial fermatas appear in brackets. Dynamic markings have been copied from the original score and/or performing parts. Where dynamic markings appear to be missing in corresponding lines they have been added in brackets.

Where a directive such as *tutti* appears in some but not all appropriate lines of the score, the directive has been added where missing without qualification if it appears in the corresponding performing part. However, if the directive is also lacking in the performing part (although it was evidently intended), it appears in the edition in brackets. Where other directives (e.g., *con l'arco* or *pizz.*) were clearly intended, they have been added in brackets.

Words that are abbreviated in the sources for spatial reasons have been written out in full without notice. Notational shorthands, such as *unis.* (appearing in full in the corresponding performing part), have been written out without comment. Repetitions of texts indicated with notational shorthand have been written out without comment. Text missing in certain lines of the score has been added from the parts without comment.

Accidentals have been placed according to modern usage; those redundant by modern standards have been tacitly deleted. Editorial accidentals appear in brackets. Cautionary accidentals are not present.

Bass figures appear below the staff in the original score.

Critical Notes

Generally, the edition follows the Sondershausen score (SSC). Information from the Sondershausen parts (SP), such as text underlay, slurs, continuo figures, or even notes in cases where they are illegible in SSC, has been added without notice unless it contradicts SSC. Adjustments for range found in the SP oboe part are adopted without notice. Information from SP that contradicts SSC is not mentioned if it is clearly an error. If a variant is rejected without reference to a source, this indicates that both SSC and SP have it. When a rejected variant in SSC only is reported, the edition adopts the variant from SP unless noted otherwise.

Parts have been abbreviated as follows: C = Canto, A = Alto, T = Tenore, B = Basso [vocal bass]; Clno. = Clarino, Timp. = Timpani, Ob. = Oboe, Vn. = Violino, Vn. Conc. = Violino Concertato, A. Va. = Alto Viola, T. Va. = Tenore Viola, Basso [instrumental bass], Cont. = Continuo, Org. = Organo [non-transposing part], Transp. Org. = transposing Organo part. In SSC the oboe and violin 1 parts (the latter of which includes the Violino Concertato) share a staff. This is rendered in the critical notes as "Ob./Vn. 1." The critical notes use the Helmholtz system of pitch notation (i.e., middle C is designated as c').

1. Herr Gott, dich loben wir

M. 3, B, note 3 is b in SSC. M. 5, A. Va., final note is g" in SSC. Mm. 7–8, B has no text in SSC; in SP it has "wir dancken dir" (repeated). M. 8, Ob./Vn. 1, note 6 is g" in SSC. Mm. 8–11, A, text underlay from m. 8, note 6 is "Herr Gott, dich loben wir" in SP. Mm. 12–13, A. Va., SSC illegible; m. 12, note 4 is g' in SP. Mm. 12–14, Vn. 2, SSC illegible at first; m. 12, note 3 is g" quarter note (tied to next bar); m. 13, notes are g" quarter note–f#" half note–e" quarter note (tied to next bar); notes in m. 14 are e" quarter note–d" half note–c#" quarter note. M. 14, A. Va., notes are c#'[?]–a#–c#' in SSC. M. 15, Clno. 3, notes 3 and 4 are 8th notes in SSC. M. 16, C, slur is over 16th notes (as elsewhere), but SSC has extraneous "wir" under the final 8th. Mm. 18–20, C, SSC has "Herr Gott dir dancken dir"; SP has "Herr Gott dich dancken dir." Mm. 20 (note 2)–22 (note 3), B, SSC has "Herr Gott dich lo-cken dir" in SSC (page break between "lo-" and "-cken"). M. 21, A, last note has "dich" in SSC. M. 22, A, last note begins "wir dancken" in SP. M. 25, C, note 3, SSC has "wir"; note 4, SSC has "dir," SP has "Herr"; A, the first two syllables are each placed one note too soon in SSC (note 3 is thus without text); note 4, SSC has "dir," SP has "Herr." M. 26, C and A, notes 1–3, SSC has "dancken wir." Mm. 27–28, A, SSC has "Gott wir loben wir." M. 29, Clno. 1, notes 6 and 7, c' 8th notes instead of 16ths in SSC, followed by only one more 8th note; C, notes 1–6, SSC has "Herr Gott dich loben wir." Mm. 29–30, T, ties missing in SSC; B, SSC has "Herr Gott dich loben wir, wir dancken dir." M. 30, T, tie missing in SP. M. 32, T, last note is d' in SSC.

2. Dich, Vater, in Ewigkeit

M. 51, Ob./Vn. 1, SSC has a" half note. M. 52, Cont., note 1, # not in SSC; within SP, only Cont. and Transp. Org. have it. M. 57, Cont., SSC has no staccato marks; within SP, only Basso has them. M. 65, Cont., note 1 is B in SSC. M. 69, Vn. 1, notes 2–3 and 4–5 slurred in SSC.

3. Heilig ist unser Gott

M. 77, Cont., erroneous tenor clef in SSC. M. 102, Timp., notes 2–4 are quarter–dotted 8th–16th in SSC. Mm. 102–4, B, SSC has "Heilig ist unser Gott, ist unser Gott." Mm. 105–7, Cont., SSC has erroneous alto clef. M. 110, Timp., notes 3–5 are quarter–dotted 8th–16th in SSC. M. 114, Clno. 1, notes 2–3 are dotted 8th and 16th in SSC. M. 124, T, SSC has a tie to m. 125. M. 127, Ob./Vn. 1, two tied half notes instead of whole note in SSC. Mm. 132–33, B, slur from last note of m. 132 to first note of m. 133 in SSC, from note 1 to note 2 of m. 133 in SP. Mm. 138–39, A. Va., slur from last note of m. 138 to first note of m. 139 in SSC. M. 143, T, note 2 is d' quarter note. M. 148, Cont., note 2, figure is 6 (not raised) in

SSC and in non-transposed Org. of SP.   M. 152, Clno. 1, note 4 lacks ♯.   M. 156, Cont., figure 2 is 6 (not raised) in SSC.   Mm. 157–58, Cont., SSC erroneously has alto clef (notes and key signature are written as if in tenor clef). M. 168, B, notes are dotted half–quarter in SP.   M. 172, Timp., notes 3–5 are quarter–dotted 8th–16th in SSC; A, SSC has "heilig ist."   M. 173, Cont., second figure is 6 (not raised) in SSC.   M. 186, C, notes are half note–8th–quarter in SSC.   M. 188, T. Va. has erroneous alto clef with key signature of a tenor clef in SSC.   Mm. 193–94, A, SSC has a tie; T. Va., SSC has two d' whole notes, tied, assuming the alto clef should be read as a tenor clef.   M. 195, Cont., SSC cumulates the notes of the parts in SP: B. and Cont. have D, Org. has d, Transp. Org. has B.

4. Dein göttlich Macht

M. 198, Ob., slur over notes 7–10 in SSC; Vn. Conc., slur over notes 7–10 in SP.   Mm. 201–2, Vn. 2 in SSC has four notes, then "unisono" in place of notes 5–13; SP has notes 5–11, then an 8th rest.   M. 205, Vn. 2, notes 1 and 2 are quarters in SSC.   Mm. 207–first half of 210 (before a page break), Cont. is not written out in SSC.   M. 210, first half (before the page break), T, SSC lacks quarter rest. M. 210, second half (after the page break), Cont., SSC has A♯ quarter, followed by a half rest–quarter rest.   Mm. 212–13, Cont., notes 5–12 are e–d–e–c♯–e–c♯–f♯ in SSC.

5. Die gantze werthe Christenheit

Mm. 218–19, Cont., upper voice lacking in Cont. and Transp. Org. of SP.   M. 221, T. Va., half rest lacks dot; Ob./Vn. 1, notes 4–5 are 8th notes instead of 16th notes in SSC; notes 8–12 are three 8ths and two 16ths in SSC. M. 223, T, note 8 is d' quarter note in SSC.   M. 224, T, note 1 is g quarter note in SSC.   M. 226, Clno. 2, last two 8th notes are e"–f" in SSC.   M. 228, A, the final syllable of "alle" appears under note 5 in SSC; thereafter there is no text until m. 230.   M. 229, A. Va., note 1 is dotted half note in SSC.   Mm. 231 and 233, C, the second syllable of "Erden" falls on note 4, the first syllable of "alle" falls on notes 5–7 in SSC.   M. 238, Cont., note 1 is B quarter note, notes 2 and 3 are dotted half–half (tied) in SSC, resulting in seven beats in the measure; possibly this means that the right hand should strike b' on beat 1, while the left hand strikes B quarter note at the same time, but the reading of SP, Org. and Transp. Org. has been preferred. M. 240, A, first half of measure has different rhythm in SSC: quarter note–half note, with underlay "al-le-"; A. Va., note 5 is a♯' in SSC.   M. 241, Clno. 3, note 3 in SSC is g'; B, SSC has b half note, g♯ half note, a quarter note, quarter rest (the first syllable of "Erden" is continued from the previous measure, with the second syllable falling on the a quarter note).   Mm. 241–43, Cont./ Basso, the note A is articulated variously in SP: both Org. parts have dotted whole notes with no ties, Cont. part has dotted half notes with a tie only between note 2 of m. 242 and note 1 of 243, Basso in SP has five dotted halves, with ties over barlines.   Mm. 242–43, Clno. 1, ties missing in SSC.   M. 245, Clno. 2, beat 3, SSC has c" 8th–c" 8th; Clno. 3, notes 3 and 4 are 16ths in SSC.   Mm. 246–47, B, syllable "al-" extends through m. 247, note 1, word not repeated.   M. 247, Timp., last note is quarter in SSC.

6. Dich, Vater, im höchsten Thron

M. 251, Cont., final rest is missing in SSC.   M. 257, T. Va., notes 1 and 2 are g♯ in SSC; B, note 3 is g in SSC. M. 260, A, rest is missing in SSC.   M. 261, Ob./Vn. 1, last note is f♯" in SSC.   M. 264, C, SSC has "Geist den." M. 266, Vn. 2, last 2 signs in SSC are 8th rest–quarter note. M. 270, A. Va., note is e' in SSC.

7. Du Kön'g der Ehren

M. 275, C, SSC has "wahr Gottes," A and B are untexted, T has "Gotts Vaters" (on notes 2–4); in SP, CATB all have "Gotts Vaters"; Cont., last note lacks ♮ in SSC.   M. 276, Clno. 1, note 9 is dotted quarter in SSC; Clno. 3, notes 1 and 2 are quarters in SSC.   M. 279, Cont., notes 8 and 9 are 8ths in SSC.   M. 281, Cont., last note lacks ♮ in SSC.   M. 282, A and A. Va., note 5 is f♯' in SSC. M. 285, T, sources have "den."   M. 287, Cont., note 8 lacks ♮; in SP, Basso, last note is replaced with e 16th–d 16th.   M. 288, Cont., lower voice not in SSC, added from B. of SP.   M. 289, Clno. 2, notes 4 and 5 are 8ths in SSC; Clno. 3, note 5 is d' in SSC.   M. 292, Cont., note 10 is d' in SSC.   M. 293, Cont. and Basso, note 8 lacks ♮.   M. 299, Cont. and Basso, note 8 lacks ♮.   M. 300, A. Va., note 2 is quarter note a' in SSC.

8. Nun hilff uns, Herr

M. 308, Vn. 2, tie is missing in SSC.   M. 309, A, note 2 has no tie; instead it has second syllable of "Dienern"; A. Va., tie is missing in SSC.   M. 310, A, note 1 has horizontal line instead of text syllable; note 2 has second syllable of "Dienern." Thus the second syllable of "Dienern" is rendered twice: once on note 2 of m. 309 and again (after a page break) on note 2 of m. 310.   M. 310, Vn. 2, tie missing in SSC.   M. 312, Ob./Vn. 1, notes are f♯"–e"– d"–c♯" in SSC, with the last three notes slurred; in SP, Ob. and Vn. 1 have the same as edition, Vn. Conc. has e"–g"– f♯"–e", with apparently the last three slurred.   M. 313, Ob./Vn. 1, notes 2 and 3 are tied in SSC (no slurs); in SP, Ob. has the same as edition, Vn. 1, notes 1 and 2 only have slur, Vn. Conc. has slur that apparently covers notes 1–3.   M. 314, Cont., figure 6 appears below note 4 instead of note 3 in SSC.   M. 315, T, note 4 is d'.   M. 316, Clno. 2, note 2 is d" in SSC, T, note 2 is a in SSC.   M. 322, Cont./Basso, SSC has whole note (tied to previous note); SP, Basso has dotted half (tied to previous note) and quarter, Org. has whole note (tied to previous note), Cont. and Transp. Org. have two half notes with first note tied to previous measure as in edition.   M. 323, B, note 3 has a tie to following measure in SSC.   Mm. 323–24, Cont., tie missing in SSC.   M. 327, CATB, note is half note. M. 330, Clno. 3, note 2 is e' in SSC, c' in SP; C, text is "ew'gen."   M. 331, all parts except A, this measure contains nothing but one half note in SSC.   M. 343, Ob./Vn. 1, note 2 is b' in SSC.   M. 351, A, note 2 lacks ♯ in SSC.

M. 352, Cont., SSC has alto clef; notes through m. 353, note 1 are notated a third too high. M. 354, C, second syllable of "aller" on note 5 in SP. M. 359, Clno. 1, five beats in measure, beat 1 is quarter rest. M. 360, Vn. 2, note 1 is e" in SSC. M. 361, Clno. 2, last note is e" in SSC. M. 363, Clno. 2, whole rest in SSC. M. 370, Ob./Vn. 1, last note is d" in SSC. M. 376, C, note 2 lacks tie in SSC. M. 377, Ob./Vn. 1, note 2 lacks tie in SSC. M. 379, A, notes 2 and 3 lack slur in SSC. M. 379, T, note 2 has tie in SSC. M. 385, C, note 2, tie with no text in SSC. M. 386, C, SSC has two half notes with text "in E-[wigkeit]." M. 396, Cont., note 1 has figure 6/5♮ in SSC. Mm. 409–10, B, SSC has "in Ewigkeit." Mm. 413, C, note 2 lacks tie in SSC. M. 415, T. Va., rest is missing in SSP; entire measure is missing in SP.

9. *Täglich, Herr Gott, wir loben dich*

M. 416, Cont. line has "Basso pizzicato. Senza organo" in SSC (with later markings indicating when the organ should enter or fall silent); SP, Basso has no instruction regarding articulation; SP, Cont. is essentially identical to SSC; SP, Org. has rests until m. 428 and continues the pattern of intermittent bars of rest; SP, Transp. Org. has "pizzicato senz' organo" (with later markings indicating when the organ should enter or fall silent). M. 419, Ob. (on separate staff here), note 5 is d" in SSC. M. 425, Vn. 1/Vn. 2, note 4 is c♯" in SSC. M. 429, Cont., extraneous quarter note B before note 1 in SSC, creating five beats in this measure. M. 432, Ob., notes 1–3 (appearing after a page break) are f♯"–e"–d" in SSC. M. 433, C, note 2, SSC has "du." M. 443, Cont., note 4 missing in SSC.

10. *Auf dich hoffen wir*

M. 451, Vn. Conc. follows Vn. 2 in SP. M. 462, Vn. 1, SSC has whole note (per unison with Ob.). M. 463, A. Va., at note 2 SSC has apparent dynamic marking: above note 2: *p:*, below note 2 on the g space of the staff: *p:*. M. 480, Ob./Vn. 1, note 2 is a' in SSC. M. 489, Cont., SSC has a tenor clef after note 1, next three pitches are notated a third too low. Mm. 495–96, T, notes 1–4, SSC divides "lie-ber" two notes per syllable, "Herr" is missing. M. 505, Vn. 2, note 2 lacks tie in SSC. M. 513, Cont., note 3 lacks ♯ in SSC. M. 514, Cont., notes 3–4 slurred in SSC. M. 519, T. Va., note 2 lacks tie in SSC.

11. *Amen*

Mm. 522–23, Ob. pitches are one octave lower in SSC and SP. M. 525, Clno. 1, notes 4–6 are all e' in SSC. M. 528, B, note 1 is half note in SSC. M. 529, A. Va., last note is a'. M. 531, C, notes 4–7 appear to be quarter–quarter–8th–8th in SSC, edition follows SP; T, note 7 is e' in SSC, edition follows the T in SP, which matches T. Va.; Vn. 2, rhythm of notes 4–7 ambiguous in SSC; SP has dotted quarter–quarter–16th–16th. Mm. 534–35, Ob., modification for range is given only for m. 535 in SP. M. 536, Ob./Vn. 1, SSC has *p* on beat 1, SP has it on beat 2; Vn. 1, notes 6–7 are a'–a' in SP. M. 539, C, note 2 has syllable "-men" on note 2 and "a-" on note 3 in SSC. M. 540, C, note 1 is b' in SSC. M. 541, Ob./Vn. 1 have *p* already on beat 3 in SSC. M. 546, Ob./Vn. 1, note 8 is b" in SP (Vn. Conc., Vn. 1, Ob.). M. 550, beats 3 and 4, lower string parts are different in SSC: Vn. 2 has d" 8th–c♯" 8th–d" 8th–8th rest; A. Va. has f♯' 8th–f♯' 8th–f♯' 8th–8th rest; T. Va. has b 8th–a 8th–b 8th–8th rest. M. 553, A, tie missing between notes 1 and 2 in SSC, but continues with previous "a-" syllable until m. 555, note 1. M. 555, C, SSC has "-men" on note 2. M. 556, A. Va., notes 3–4 are quarters in SSC. M. 566, A, note 4 is missing in SSC. M. 567, T. Va., note 3 lacks ♯ in SSC. M. 572, B, note 3, SSC has extraneous syllable "a-." M. 576, Ob./Vn. 1, notes 1–4 are c♯"–a'–a'–d' in SSC; Basso, note 5 is G in SP; similarly, Cont. and Transp. Org. have G and E respectively in SP. M. 577, C, note 3 is c♯" in SSC. M. 578, A. Va., notes 3–4 are quarters in SSC, edition follows SP (doubling A). M. 579, Ob./Vn. 1, notes 2 and 3 are both a' in SP. M. 580, Clno. 2, note 3 is quarter in SP. Mm. 580, 582, Basso has ties in SP. Mm. 580–83, several variants in SP: Cont. ties all notes; Org. has no ties; Transp. Org. has tie in m. 580. M. 583, T, notes 1–2 have "-men, a-" in SSC. M. 585, Clno. 2, note 2 lacks tie in SSC. M. 586, Clno. 2, final note is d" in SP. M. 587, B, note 1 is half note.

Recent Researches in the Music of the Baroque Era
Christoph Wolff, general editor

Vol.	Composer: Title
1	Marc-Antoine Charpentier: *Judicium Salomonis*
2	Georg Philipp Telemann: *Forty-eight Chorale Preludes*
3	Johann Caspar Kerll: *Missa Superba*
4–5	Jean-Marie Leclair: *Sonatas for Violin and Basso continuo, Opus 5*
6	*Ten Eighteenth-Century Voluntaries*
7–8	William Boyce: *Two Anthems for the Georgian Court*
9	Giulio Caccini: *Le nuove musiche*
10–11	Jean-Marie Leclair: *Sonatas for Violin and Basso continuo, Opus 9 and Opus 15*
12	Johann Ernst Eberlin: *Te Deum; Dixit Dominus; Magnificat*
13	Gregor Aichinger: *Cantiones Ecclesiasticae*
14–15	Giovanni Legrenzi: *Cantatas and Canzonets for Solo Voice*
16	Giovanni Francesco Anerio and Francesco Soriano: *Two Settings of Palestrina's "Missa Papae Marcelli"*
17	Giovanni Paolo Colonna: *Messe a nove voci concertata con stromenti*
18	Michel Corrette: *"Premier livre d'orgue" and "Nouveau livre de noëls"*
19	Maurice Greene: *Voluntaries and Suites for Organ and Harpsichord*
20	Giovanni Antonio Piani: *Sonatas for Violin Solo and Violoncello with Cembalo*
21–22	Marin Marais: *Six Suites for Viol and Thoroughbass*
23–24	Dario Castello: *Selected Ensemble Sonatas*
25	*A Neapolitan Festa a Ballo and Selected Instrumental Ensemble Pieces*
26	Antonio Vivaldi: *The Manchester Violin Sonatas*
27	Louis-Nicolas Clérambault: *Two Cantatas for Soprano and Chamber Ensemble*
28	Giulio Caccini: *Nuove musiche e nuova maniera di scriverle (1614)*
29–30	Michel Pignolet de Montéclair: *Cantatas for One and Two Voices*
31	Tomaso Albinoni: *Twelve Cantatas, Opus 4*
32–33	Antonio Vivaldi: *Cantatas for Solo Voice*
34	Johann Kuhnau: *Magnificat*
35	Johann Stadlmayr: *Selected Magnificats*
36–37	Jacopo Peri: *Euridice: An Opera in One Act, Five Scenes*
38	Francesco Severi: *Salmi passaggiati (1615)*
39	George Frideric Handel: *Six Concertos for the Harpsichord or Organ (Walsh's Transcriptions, 1738)*
40	*The Brasov Tablature (Brasov Music Manuscript 808): German Keyboard Studies 1608–1684*
41	John Coprario: *Twelve Fantasias for Two Bass Viols and Organ and Eleven Pieces for Three Lyra Viols*

42	Antonio Cesti: *Il pomo d'oro (Music for Acts III and V from Modena, Biblioteca Estense, Ms. Mus. E. 120)*
43	Tomaso Albinoni: *Pimpinone: Intermezzi comici musicali*
44–45	Antonio Lotti: *Duetti, terzetti, e madrigali a piu voci*
46	Matthias Weckmann: *Four Sacred Concertos*
47	Jean Gilles: *Requiem (Messe des morts)*
48	Marc-Antoine Charpentier: *Vocal Chamber Music*
49	*Spanish Art Song in the Seventeenth Century*
50	Jacopo Peri: *"Le varie musiche" and Other Songs*
51–52	Tomaso Albinoni: *Sonatas and Suites, Opus 8, for Two Violins, Violoncello, and Basso continuo*
53	Agostino Steffani: *Twelve Chamber Duets*
54–55	Gregor Aichinger: *The Vocal Concertos*
56	Giovanni Battista Draghi: *Harpsichord Music*
57	*Concerted Sacred Music of the Bologna School*
58	Jean-Marie Leclair: *Sonatas for Violin and Basso continuo, Opus 2*
59	Isabella Leonarda: *Selected Compositions*
60–61	Johann Schelle: *Six Chorale Cantatas*
62	Denis Gaultier: *La Rhétorique des Dieux*
63	Marc-Antoine Charpentier: *Music for Molière's Comedies*
64–65	Georg Philipp Telemann: *Don Quichotte auf der Hochzeit des Comacho: Comic Opera-Serenata in One Act*
66	Henry Butler: *Collected Works*
67–68	John Jenkins: *The Lyra Viol Consorts*
69	*Keyboard Transcriptions from the Bach Circle*
70	Melchior Franck: *Geistliche Gesäng und Melodeyen*
71	Georg Philipp Telemann: *Douze solos, à violon ou traversière*
72	Marc-Antoine Charpentier: *Nine Settings of the "Litanies de la Vierge"*
73	*The Motets of Jacob Praetorius II*
74	Giovanni Porta: *Selected Sacred Music from the Ospedale della Pietà*
75	*Fourteen Motets from the Court of Ferdinand II of Hapsburg*
76	Jean-Marie Leclair: *Sonatas for Violin and Basso continuo, Opus 1*
77	Antonio Bononcini: *Complete Sonatas for Violoncello and Basso continuo*
78	Christoph Graupner: *Concerti Grossi for Two Violins*
79	Paolo Quagliati: *Il primo libro de' madrigali a quattro voci*
80	Melchior Franck: *Dulces Mundani Exilij Deliciae*
81	*Late-Seventeenth-Century English Keyboard Music*
82	*Solo Compositions for Violin and Viola da gamba with Basso continuo*
83	Barbara Strozzi: *Cantate, ariete a una, due e tre voci, Opus 3*
84	Charles-Hubert Gervais: *Super flumina Babilonis*

85	Henry Aldrich: *Selected Anthems and Motet Recompositions*
86	Lodovico Grossi da Viadana: *Salmi a quattro cori*
87	Chiara Margarita Cozzolani: *Motets*
88	Elisabeth-Claude Jacquet de La Guerre: *Cephale et Procris*
89	Sébastien Le Camus: *Airs à deux et trois parties*
90	Thomas Ford: *Lyra Viol Duets*
91	*Dedication Service for St. Gertrude's Chapel, Hamburg, 1607*
92	Johann Klemm: *Partitura seu Tabulatura italica*
93	Giovanni Battista Somis: *Sonatas for Violin and Basso continuo, Opus 3*
94	John Weldon: *The Judgment of Paris*
95–96	Juan Bautista Comes: *Masses. Parts 1–2*
97	Sebastian Knüpfer: *Lustige Madrigalien und Canzonetten*
98	Stefano Landi: *La morte d'Orfeo*
99	Giovanni Battista Fontana: *Sonatas for One, Two, and Three Parts with Basso continuo*
100	Georg Philipp Telemann: *Twelve Trios*
101	Fortunato Chelleri: *Keyboard Music*
102	Johann David Heinichen: *La gara degli Dei*
103	Johann David Heinichen: *Diana su l'Elba*
104	Alessandro Scarlatti: *Venere, Amore e Ragione*
105	*Songs with Theorbo (ca. 1650–1663)*
106	Melchior Franck: *Paradisus Musicus*
107	Heinrich Ignaz Franz von Biber: *Missa Christi resurgentis*
108	Johann Ludwig Bach: *Motets*
109–10	Giovanni Rovetta: *Messa, e salmi concertati, op. 4 (1639). Parts 1–2*
111	Johann Joachim Quantz: *Seven Trio Sonatas*
112	Petits motets *from the Royal Convent School at Saint Cyr*
113	Isabella Leonarda: *Twelve Sonatas, Opus 16*
114	Rudolph di Lasso: *Virginalia Eucharistica (1615)*
115	Giuseppe Torelli: *Concerti musicali, Opus 6*
116–17	Nicola Francesco Haym: *Complete Sonatas. Parts 1–2*
118	Benedetto Marcello: *Il pianto e il riso delle quattro stagioni*
119	Loreto Vittori: *La Galatea*
120–23	William Lawes: *Collected Vocal Music. Parts 1–4*
124	Marco da Gagliano: *Madrigals. Part 1*
125	Johann Schop: *Erster Theil newer Paduanen*
126	Giovanni Felice Sances: *Motetti a una, due, tre, e quattro voci (1638)*
127	Thomas Elsbeth: *Sontägliche Evangelien*
128–30	Giovanni Antonio Rigatti: *Messa e salmi, parte concertati. Parts 1–3*
131	*Seventeenth-Century Lutheran Church Music with Trombones*

132	Francesco Cavalli: *La Doriclea*
133	*Music for "Macbeth"*
134	Domenico Allegri: *Music for an Academic Defense (Rome, 1617)*
135	Jean Gilles: *Diligam te, Domine*
136	Silvius Leopold Weiss: *Lute Concerti*
137	*Masses by Alessandro Scarlatti and Francesco Gasparini*
138	Giovanni Ghizzolo: *Madrigali et arie per sonare et cantare*
139	Michel Lambert: *Airs from "Airs de différents autheurs"*
140	William Babell: *Twelve Solos for a Violin or Oboe with Basso Continuo. Book 1*
141	Giovanni Francesco Anerio: *Selva armonica (Rome, 1617)*
142–43	Bellerofonte Castaldi: *Capricci (1622). Parts 1–2*
144	Georg von Bertouch: *Sonatas a 3*
145	Marco da Gagliano: *Madrigals. Part 2*
146	Giovanni Rovetta: *Masses*
147	Giacomo Antonio Perti: *Five-Voice Motets for the Assumption of the Virgin Mary*
148	Giovanni Felice Sances: *Motetti a 2, 3, 4, e cinque voci (1642)*
149	*La grand-mére amoureuse, parodie d'Atys*
150	Andreas Hammerschmidt: *Geistlicher Dialogen Ander Theil*
151	Georg von Bertouch: *Three Sacred Cantatas*
152	Giovanni Maria Ruggieri: *Two Settings of the Gloria*
153	Alessandro Scarlatti: *Concerti sacri, opera seconda*
154	Johann Sigismund Kusser: *Adonis*
155	John Blow: *Selected Verse Anthems*
156	Anton Holzner: *Viretum pierium (1621)*
157	Alessandro Scarlatti: *Venere, Adone, et Amore*
158	Marc-Antoine Charpentier: *In nativitatem Domini canticum, H. 416*
159	Francesco Scarlatti: *Six Concerti Grossi*
160	Charles Avison: *Concerto Grosso Arrangements of Geminiani's Opus 1 Violin Sonatas*
161	Johann David Heinichen: *Selected Music for Vespers*
162–63	Francesco Gasparini: *Cantatas with Violins. Parts 1–2*
164–65	Antoine Boesset: *Sacred Music. Parts 1–2*
166	Andreas Hammerschmidt: *Selections from the "Gespräche" (1655–56) with Capellen*
167	Santiago de Murcia: *Cifras selectas de guitarra.*
168	Gottfried Heinrich Stölzel: *German Te Deum*

Of Related Interest

Andreas Hammerschmidt, *Selections from the "Gespräche" (1655–56) with Capellen*, edited by Charlotte A. Leonard, Recent Researches in the Music of the Baroque Era, 166

Georg von Bertouch, *Three Sacred Cantatas*, edited by Michael W. Nordbakke, Recent Researches in the Music of the Baroque Era, 151

Andreas Hammerschmidt, *Geistlicher Dialogen Ander Theil*, edited by Janette Tilley, Recent Researches in the Music of the Baroque Era, 150

For more information about these or any other volumes, see our website:
http://www.areditions.com/rr/

A-R Editions, Inc.

Middleton, Wisconsin
800 736-0070 (North American book orders)
608 836-9000 (phone)
608 831-8200 (fax)
http://www.areditions.com

ISBN 978-0-89579-677-6